Hey Look...
I Made a Book!

D0838986

Hey Look...
I Made a Book!

~

Betty Doty &
Rebecca Meredith

Ten Speed Press

🏃

Ten Speed Press
P.O. Box 7123
Berkeley, California 94707

Illustrations on pages 74, 75, and 76 by
Jo Friedlund Murphy; illustration on page 21 by
Brooke Meredith; all other illustrations by
Susan Pinkerton Lehmberg.

Library of Congress Cataloging-in-Publication Data

Doty, Betty.
Hey look—I made a book! / Betty Doty and Rebecca Meredith.
p. cm
Includes bibliographical references and index.
ISBN 0-89815-686-6 : $7.95
1. Book design. 2. Bookbinding. 3. Book ornamentation.
I. Meredith, Rebecca, 1952–   . II. Title.
Z116.A3D68 1995   94-48351
686.3'5—dc20   CIP

1   2   3   4   5   —   98   97   96   95   94

to all of us who have ever felt the thrill of opening a new book...

~ CONTENTS ~

1 The Possibilities   1

2 Is Handbinding Easy?   3

3 Ideas for Blank Books   5

4 Putting Printed Pages Inside   13

5 Gathering the Materials   24

6 Binding Hardbound Books   34

7 Making Multiple Copies of Printed Books   69

8 Suggestions for Group Projects   89

9 A Word About Publishing   101

   Index   117

   Order Form   119

1

THE POSSIBILITIES

You've taken this little book in your hands, and you're probably trying to figure out what it's all about.

Hmmm...instructions for binding hardbound books...

Now your mind is whirling with ideas:

Personalized blank books as gifts? Would they be easy to make? And fun?

Gluing isn't too hard, and hand sewing is easy. I can already see a stack of blank books before me—in all colors, shapes, and sizes.

Wait a minute: If I can make a blank book, I can also use a copy machine and print out recipes, poems, and stories. I can make dozens of copies of my own handbound books.

And I bet all the instructions I'll need are in my hands—right this minute.

2

Is Handbinding Easy?

*M*aybe you're still flipping through these pages, just savoring the thought of creating a hardbound book.

Here's a safe prediction: Some of you will soon discover that handbinding hardbound books is actually easy.

At each step of the process, we think you'll be continually amazed to find that no special skill is needed. Even the sewing only entails pushing a needle and thread through holes you've punched in advance.

If bookbinding is so easy, you may be

wondering why more people aren't doing it. We think there's an easy answer: Good instructions and the necessary materials haven't been easily available.

We'll be helping you in both of these areas. We'll make our instructions as clear as we can, and we also offer packets of precut materials by mail (see page 119 for order form).

But for those of you who prefer to gather and prepare materials on your own, you'll find all the information you'll need right here.

3

IDEAS FOR BLANK BOOKS

*A*h creativity...brainstorming...just thinking about making blank books…. What fun.

Once we were quoted as saying that we hadn't been able to cover a book with rabbit fur. You can guess what we found in the mail one day: A book that was white, furry, and beautiful.

Naturally, we're wondering what would happen if we said we're having trouble making a book covered with gold and precious jewels. (Just kidding? Not really!)

Half the fun of bookmaking is deciding the

purpose for each book. For starters, consider this:

§ Let's say you plan to give a friend a bon voyage present. And you want it small enough to go inside an overpacked bag. Aha! You can find a map of your friend's destination and use it to cover a little book. Just right for the most personal notes.

§ Uncle Henry is the family joke teller, and he'd probably like a book larger than this one, maybe double the size. Then he could add sketches as he's writing out his jokes. His book would be dark colored and rugged looking, maybe even with a soft leatherette cover so it could be crammed into his jacket pocket.

§ Evidently we like a peek into each other's kitchens, hence the popularity of cookbooks that contain personal comments. For cooks who keep notes while they're working, maybe a blank book could be covered with vinyl (shelf paper?). Then the notes could easily be found again (as such a book would certainly earn a special place in any kitchen).

§ Aunt Liz likes things that are small, so it might be fun to experiment with making miniature books...say a thumbnail sketchbook, the size of a thumbnail?

§ For a Scottish friend, a book could be bound with the tartan of the family clan. For one who's Irish, something in green. For Italians, maybe a scrap from a red, white, and green tablecloth. Ooooh, what stereotypes...maybe we'd better go in another direction.

§ How about books to go with occupations? No, no, not a book covered with a greasy cloth for a mechanic...or a red-splotched bandage for a nurse....

But you know how brainstorming works. At first you just let the ideas come out. There's gotta be a few good ones...somewhere. Oops! Once our flow of brainstorms started we couldn't get them stopped. So we're offering just a few more ideas for making personalized blank books:

§ You could create your own birthday book to hold notes made on your birthday each year. (It would be easy to make the cover special with embroidery, appliqué, or cross-stitch.)

When your friends are admiring your exciting creation, you might offer to teach them bookbinding. Or maybe your thinking goes more like this: Why don't I use this book as a guide, order materials, then invite some friends over so all of us can learn bookbinding together?

§ If you enjoy hosting get-togethers, an attractive book might be used for noting guest lists for each special festivity...with reminders of what went right or wrong. Maybe the book could become a permanent checklist (with preparation times) for future entertaining.

§ For a Valentine's Day gift, you might make an extra-special book covered in velour, warm and soft (just in case that's the feeling you're trying to convey).

§ Maybe a grandparent or someone else in your family often talks about writing out favorite family stories (or maybe poems?) but no action is taken. It's possible that all the motivation your relative needs to get started on such a project might simply be to receive an especially beautiful book from you. The book's cover could match the curtains—or wallpaper?—of a favorite family hideaway.

❧ You could give books instead of get-well cards. Not only would they be great for keeping records (or doodling, or whatever comes with the convalescing), but a book cover could easily be personalized for one particular time and place (the year of the crutches?).

❧ When thinking of children, it's as if another layer of the brainstorming cells is shaken loose. You can make books with washable covers (Scotchgard?) and write out a child's personalized story. Or for an especially treasured ABC book, the child might name ABC objects over a period of time, and you might make sketches as the ideas come in.

❧ You can make blank books with a favorite photograph in a padded frame on the book's cover. (Then the trick would be figuring out how to put a strip of cardboard on the back of the book so it could be displayed standing upright.)

❧ What about a wedding gift, maybe a book made well in advance of the wedding? Then the book could be passed around to friends and relatives who would record their best advice for a successful marriage. Or what about making a sign-in book for a wedding ceremony?

That's enough. We'd better put our brainstorming genie back in the bottle and put the cork on...tight.

4

PUTTING
PRINTED PAGES INSIDE

$\mathcal{M}$any of us walk around with unwritten books in our heads. And some of us will get them out before we die.

For us, the pleasure of learning bookbinding isn't only making blank books. It's also knowing that we can use a copy machine and create books for readers' consideration—any time we choose.

No doubt you've learned what we have, that it really isn't easy to get our ideas across to others. How different it would be if we could read each other's books, the books pro-duced in solitude while we're each trying to figure out exactly what we want to say and exactly how to say it.

Unlike thinking and talking, while writing we're trying to slow down a whirling brain so our words can stand still. It's a never-ending process of trying to rescue one thought at a time from a fleeting mass, then isolating just the right word so we can best express what's most important to us...at that second.

We have a friend who used to tell us, every time we'd see him, that he was working on the Great American Novel. In later years, he'd chuckle before telling us he was working on the Great American Sentence. Now his humor is in full force. He says he's working on the Great American Word. (Hmmm… before we print this, wonder if we should phone him to see if he'll say he's working on the Great American Letter.)

We're assuming that some of you fellow booklovers have a manuscript or two hidden away in a drawer somewhere. From what we know about publishing, it's easy to believe that you might have become discouraged about getting your work out.

Be prepared for a change. Maybe your best ideas will soon be seeing the light of day. Did you know that some self-published books have gone all the way to the top of the bestseller list? One of them, *What Color Is Your Parachute?* by Richard Nelson Bolles, was on the bestseller list for 280 weeks. And over five million copies have now been sold.

Just from reading this book, you may go into the publishing business. After we give bookbinding instructions (in the next two chapters), we'll show how to lay out printed pages (chapter 7) and how to begin publishing (chapter 9).

As we're writing this book, we keep thinking about printed pages. But we're not forgetting that your "thing" might be music or art.

Duet for Clarinet and Viola

We'll finish this chapter by offering suggestions for practicing making books, maybe as gifts for starters. This will give you a chance to check out our instructions before deciding to create your own *magnum opus*.

§ Creating personalized calendars or address books could be fun, especially if you're making up your own quotes to sprinkle throughout.

§ You might want to preserve memories of a recent family get-together, all hardbound and ready to present to each family member.

§ A fairly simple book to make would be mostly blank except that it could have a family member's quote at the bottom of each page.

Grandma B: "Success isn't getting what we want; it's wanting what we get."

Aunt Suzy: "The only thing we can be an expert on is our own opinion."

Uncle Ted: (who brought this back from Japan): "It isn't good to bite your navel."

§ Children's artwork is so often lost because of sheer bulk. Why not preserve the best samples (shrunk or stretched by copy machine) in hardbound books to circulate within the family?

Thousands of elementary school students have learned the pleasures of handbinding blank books by using the methods presented in this book. For a long-range project, the following idea may suggest some interesting variations for teachers and group leaders.

An archeologist told us that he was having trouble getting the results published of his recent excavation. He was excavating a local Indian lookout site, which just happened to be near an elementary school. The archeologist was wondering if students (with considerable adult help) might compile the information...and then bind books to be used in classrooms each year.

For this particular project, there's also the possibility of selling books. The Indian lookout site is at the top of a valley where three mountain ranges come together. A freeway and shops are close by, and it's easy to guess that the books would be appreciated by both nearby residents and travelers.

Maybe your mind is bulging with ideas about possible books. Yet you may have been assuming that book production was the exclusive territory of big publishers (who need big markets and big profits). What if there are unexplored spaces, out there some-where, just waiting for people like us?

5

GATHERING THE MATERIALS

*E*arlier, we said that many people don't bind books because it's not that easy to get the right materials.

We're hoping to save you frustration (and money, too) by offering packets of materials for books this size. Later we'll show how you can gather and prepare materials for books of all sizes. But first we'll list the materials you need to make a hardbound book the size of this one, except that yours will have a few more pages (140 instead of 128 pages).

44" of white carpet-and-button thread

Darning needle

1 24"-long strip of wax paper

2 tablespoons of a white glue called padding cement. It can be purchased from an office supply store or print shop. It has the flexibility needed for the book's spine. Be sure to get the kind that's washable and non-toxic. To get the amount you'll need for one book, the minimum you may be able to buy is a quart (about $15).

1 7" x 10½" piece of medium-weight cloth. After you've practiced your bookbinding for a while, you may "graduate" to using heavier or lighter material. As you can guess, for lightweight material you need an extra-thin coat of glue so it won't show through.

70-pound book paper for pages. Sixty pound is also good. (Most copy machine paper is 20-pound bond.) There seems to be an almost unbelievable variety of paper (and descriptions thereof) available. But what's important is that the paper be heavy enough that the ink doesn't bleed through to the other side when you write on the pages.

To be sure your book lasts 30 years or more, ask your printer/stationer about acid-free paper. You also may want to request recycled paper. And some of you crafters may even try handmade paper. We found we had to use spray starch on handmade paper before we could write on it, but it made a beautiful book.

One ream of paper, 500 sheets, makes 28 books. You may be able to buy just a few sheets at a copy shop. The current price of

70-pound book stock ranges from $6 to $25 or more per ream.

To make a 140-page book, you'd start with 17½ sheets of standard 8½" x 11" paper. Cut them in half so you'll have 35 sheets 8½" x 5½". When you fold them in the middle you'll have 140 pages 5½" x 4¼". (If you think of one 8½" x 11" sheet folded in quarters, you can see that there are 4 pages on each side. A two-sided sheet would give you 8 pages, so 17½ sheets would make 140 pages.)

1 sheet of any kind of white paper, cut to 5¾" x 9½", for the cover guide. The 9½" may be altered slightly for heavier or thinner cover fabrics. This paper cover guide won't show in the finished book.

Paper for the end papers. This is optional. End papers are glued just inside front and back covers and are usually made out of parchment paper. They're cut the same size as the paper used for the book pages (5½" x 8½").

Cardboard (called chipboard), ³/₃₂" **thick**. This is hard to find and hard to cut. But the thickness is needed as a precaution against warping. You may be able to find it in a picture framing shop or an art supply or engineering supply store. (And it's possible you can cut it with a paper cutter there.) Front and back covers are 5¾" x 4¼", and the spine is 5¾" x ⁷/₁₆".

Now, about making books of different sizes:

1. First, decide what size you want your pages to be.

2. Determine the size of the cover cardboard this way:

- For height, cut cardboard $1/4$" taller than the pages.

- For width, cut cardboard the same as the width of the pages.

- Before you figure the spine width, you'll need to read the instructions in the next chapter, page 34.

3. Measure cover guide for books of all sizes this way:

- The height of the cover guide is the same as the height of the pages.

- To figure the width, lay the 2 covers and spine out flat with $1/8$" space

on each side of the spine. The total
of the width of the cardboard and
spaces determines the width of the
cover guide you'll need.

4. To determine the size of the cover cloth for
any book, lay out your cloth with the
cover guide on top. Then trim cloth to
allow $\frac{1}{2}$" margins all around.

Materials Checklist

❏ Thread

❏ Glue

❏ Needle

❏ Cloth

❏ Wax paper

❏ Paper for pages

❏ Paper for cover guide

❏ Paper for 2 end papers (optional)

❏ Cardboard for cover and spines

There are also a few materials you'll need that aren't provided in our materials packet (or listed earlier):

❒ Ruler (optional)

❒ Pencil

❒ Dish to hold glue

❒ Scissors

❒ Scratch paper or paper towels

❒ Clothespins or metal clamps

❒ Brush to apply glue

A 1"-wide sponge brush is good, but take special care to keep from applying too much glue. If you're going to make very many books, especially books that are oversized, we hope you'll treat yourself to a 3" paint roller (about $3 from a paint store). It's great for applying thin, even coats of glue. The roller comes with a plastic tray to hold the glue.

6

BINDING HARDBOUND BOOKS

Step 1: Folding Pages

*T*o make a 140-page hardbound book, divide the 35 sheets (5$\frac{1}{2}$" x 8$\frac{1}{2}$") into 7 stacks of 5 sheets.

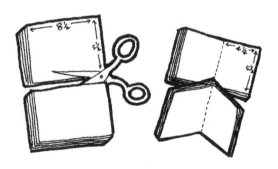

Then take each stack of sheets and fold them in half. This group of folded sheets is called a signature.

Notice that when you fold the sheets the edges are uneven. This is the way all books were until a few years ago. You'll still want to make the folded pages as neat—and as tightly creased—as you can. When you've folded all the sheets into groups of 5, you'll have 7 signatures. (Starting with this step is especially good if you're working with a group. Doing something so easy and "fool-proof" gives everyone a chance to relax and get comfortable before moving on.)

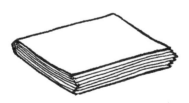

When making books of different sizes, here's how you figure the cardboard for the spine: Squeeze together the pages at the folds and measure. The spine should be cut the exact width of the tightly squeezed-together signatures.

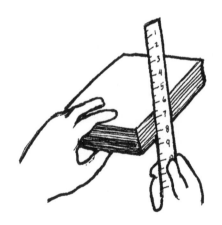

Step 2: Joining Cardboards to Cover Guide

Lay out the cover guide, and on top of it lay out the 3 cardboards with the spine in the middle.

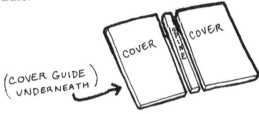

Glue each piece in place, doing the spine last, after applying a thin, even coat of glue. When applying glue to the cardboards, it helps to lay them on a piece of scrap paper so the glue can easily be applied all the way to the edge. (Don't use the wax paper for this step because you'll need it clean for later.)

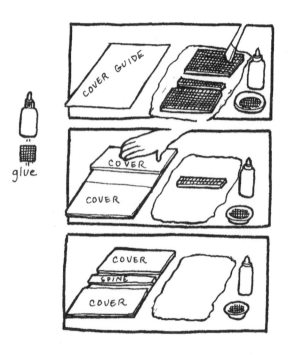

glue

Step 3:
Gluing the Cardboards and
Cover Guide to the Cover Cloth

Next you'll apply a thin, even coat of glue on top of the cardboard. Then turn the glued side onto the wrong side of the cover cloth. Leave about ½" cloth margins on all sides.

½" margins

Look at the right side of the attached cloth and check to see that it's smooth. (The cover cloth doesn't need to be ironed in advance as you'll smooth it out when glued.)

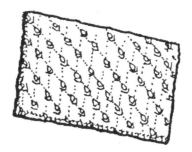

Trim excess cloth margins to about ³/₈".

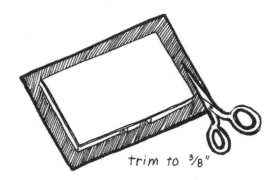

trim to ³/₈"

Put a small amount of glue in each corner of the cover guide, and turn the cloth corners over to make neat 45° angles.

You may need to hold the corners down with your fingers (or you can use clothespins protected with scraps of wax paper) until the glue holds. For heavy material it helps to use a glue gun.

Turn the cloth top margin down making a 45° angle at the corners.

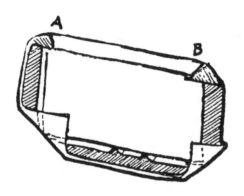

We suggest you double, double check to see that the cover is pulled tight to the cardboard. Two spots—marked A and B— require special care. Be sure your book doesn't have a corner like this...

Part of the pleasure—and pain—of book-binding is that *everyone* knows what a book is supposed to look like.

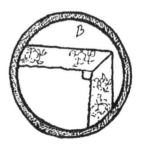

Turn the bottom margin up, following all the same instructions, especially keeping an eye on points C and D.

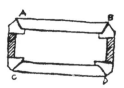

Finish by gluing the cover material to the sides, this time especially watching points W and X and Y and Z. Use clothespins and wax paper whenever necessary.

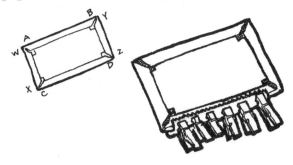

Turn the cover over (and admire it) and check to see that the corners are truly square. Because the glue is still tacky, you can do some correcting if necessary.

If you want, you can put a crease on each side of the spine so you can visualize your finished book.

Step 4: Preparing the Pages for Sewing

Take the folded signatures and stack them as if they were in a book, with the folds toward you.

Use a pencil to mark across the folded edges this way: Squeeze the signatures together and run a pencil across the folds to draw 4 lines as shown. One line is approximately $1/2''$ from each end, and 2 lines are drawn in the middle. (For a book double this size, you may want to make 6 marks.)

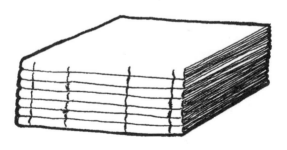

Punch holes for sewing by opening each signature, laying it out flat, then punching a needle hole through each pencil mark. (The punching may be easier if you do it over a crack in the table.)

Here's an extra touch if you're doing books in quantity: Punch a needle into a cork to provide a handle for your punch.

Restack the signatures with the folds toward you, and **make sure the holes line up straight.**

Then write the word TOP on the top signature. (You won't have to erase this later as it will soon be covered with glue.)

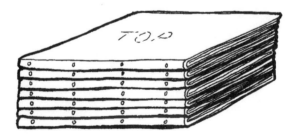

Thread your needle with the 44"-long thread and put a knot about 2" from the end of the thread.

KNOT

2" TAIL

For those inexperienced in handling a needle and thread, it's wise to put a small amount of glue on the thread as shown. This keeps the needle from coming unthreaded while sewing. You can easily cut off the glued-together thread later.

Step 5: Sewing

This chart shows the folded signatures indicated by a, b, c, and so on. The numbers indicate the needle holes in the folds, which are facing you. The drawing shows the order in which you'll be entering each pre-punched hole.

If you'll look at each number in the drawing, in order from 1 to 40, you'll easily figure out the sewing pattern. Take plenty of time. Getting comfortable with this preliminary overview of the sewing will make everything easier for you.

Notice that the middle holes have two numbers to show that each needle hole is entered twice.

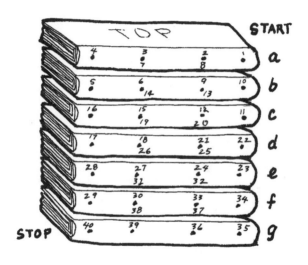

A thick book is made exactly the same as a thin one. Each signature is merely fastened to the one before. You never go back more than one signature.

Top signature a: Push the needle into the signature from the outside, starting at the right-hand needle hole. Go under to hole 2, over to hole 3, and under and out of the signature at hole 4.

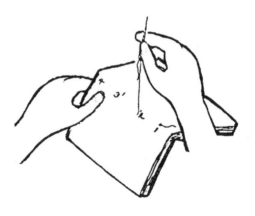

Signature b: Place this signature below the first (with TOP on top) and be sure the pencil marks are lining up. Then enter signature b from the outside (hole 5) and go under and come out at hole 6... and STOP.

It is sometimes helpful to put a clothespin at that point where you see the left hand holding the two signatures in the drawing to remind you which two signatures you're working with.

(Remember that you never work with more than two signatures at a time. And another tip: You always enter any signature, for the first time, from the outside of the fold.)

After you pause at hole 6, you're ready to join signature b to the TOP signature by way of the two middle holes. Go from hole 6 (over the outside of the folds) and enter hole 7. Go under to hole 8, then back to hole 9 on signature b. You'll then go under the fold to come out of the signature at hole 10.

Pull the thread so the signatures are firmly connected (but not too tight, because you may need a little "give" later). At this point, tie your long thread to the tail below the knot.

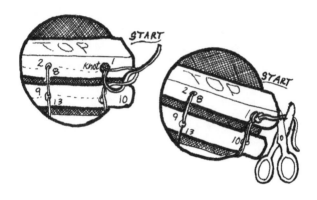

Trim off the excess thread **below the knot only**. When working with children, you might need to be extra vigilant to make sure they cut the thread in the right place.

Signature c: Be sure TOP is on top, and place signature c below b. Line up the needle holes and go from hole 10 over to hole 11 (in signature c), then under and come out through hole 12. Go over the top to hole 13 (in signature b) then under to hole 14. Come back to signature c at hole 15, then go under to point 16...and STOP.

At hole 16, the only thing new is that you'll make a loop and pull your needle through it. (This makes a half hitch and it fastens the ends of signatures b and c together.)

Follow the numbers on the chart, and you'll see that you use half hitches to join signature ends at holes 22, 28, and 34. At hole 40, use 2 half hitches...and your sewing is complete.

Half-hitches at circled numbers

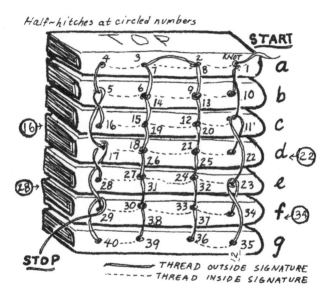

THREAD OUTSIDE SIGNATURE
THREAD INSIDE SIGNATURE

— 57 —

Step 6: Gluing the Spine

Hold the sewn signatures in your hand, then tap the folds so the top and bottom of the pages are even. (Children tend to overdo this tapping a little, but that's all right because it's an important step.)

With the folds up, carefully put 2 clothes-pins on as shown.

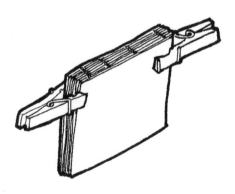

Apply a light coat of glue across the folds. To make sure the pages stay even as the glue dries, put several clothespins (prevent sticking by using wax paper) on top of the spine.

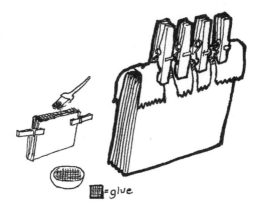

■ = glue

The glue stays tacky a while, so you can do whatever is necessary to keep the back of the spine flat and the tops and bottoms of the pages even.

Let the glue dry, maybe 10 minutes or so. It's true, however, that your book might not suffer too much if you let it dry a shorter time.

When you're a pro at bookbinding, you may do your sewing first then make the cover while the glue dries. We reversed the order because we think it's more fun to see how great the cover looks before doing the sewing.

Step 7: Attaching Sewn Pages to the Cover and Doing the Finishing Touches

Apply an even coat of glue to the page marked TOP. (Use a scrap of paper under the TOP page so you can get glue all the way to the edges.)

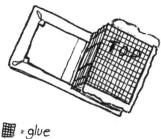

▦ = glue

You may want to stand up for the next step, because it will be easier to see exactly where you want to attach this glued sheet to the front cover. Use your eye to determine how it should look (with about $\frac{1}{8}$" margins around the edge) and just lay down the glued sheet.

Smooth down this glued page carefully.

Lay a clean piece of wax paper between the newly glued page and the rest of the book, then close the book.

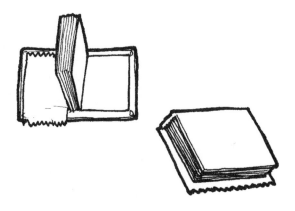

Ignore the spine area as it will take care of itself.

Apply glue (with a scrap of paper underneath) to the last page.

You may want to stand again as you fit this glued page to the back cover. Gently pull the sheet so it makes the $1/8$" margins. (This is the most scary step, but the reward is great.)

Smooth down the glued page carefully, and insert a piece of clean wax paper before closing the book.

When you stop admiring your work, carefully cup the book's spine in one hand and, with the other hand, gently push the signatures back into the spine area. Close the book as you push.

If you want a crease between the spine and the cover, make it with your fingernail.

You can take the wax paper out to admire your book, but be sure to get it back—soon.

Put the book (along with the wax paper) under a heavy weight and leave it for a day or two. (Yes, you can safely take it out at intervals...or whenever someone begs to see it.)

End papers are optional and you can add them to the front and back of the book any time. End papers are especially good to use in books with heavy cover material (such as velour or fur cloth), because the end papers minimize the heaviness of the material.

Simply glue the 2 sheets in as shown, fitting the paper exactly on top of the first and last glued-down pages.

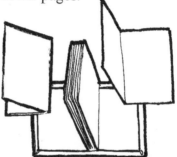

Add a narrow strip of glue to the adjoining page. You'll notice this is the way end papers are in other books.

When you're finished with your first book we predict you'll be amazed, pleased with yourself, and excited.

7

MAKING
MULTIPLE COPIES OF
PRINTED BOOKS

*A*fter learning basic bookbinding, it's no problem to bind printed pages instead of blank ones. All that's new is:

- making sure the pages are in the right order before sewing the signatures

- laying out each page the way you want it

Because there are so many different methods of getting your work in print, we're going to by-pass that discussion entirely. We suspect that readers will range from those constantly dazzled by computerized creations to those who dream of producing tiny hand-lettered masterpieces with homemade soybean ink and a quill pen.

Step 1 :
Making a First Dummy of
Your Book

Let's say your manuscript (or book plans) are complete. Now, what you want is to get a tentative idea of how the book will look.

Once you've decided the size of your pages, fold the sheets of blank paper to make them into signatures (usually 5 sheets each).

Keep folding and guessing about the number of pages and signatures you'll need.

Number each page, and we'll call these your original numbers.

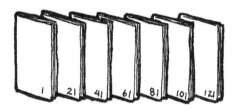

Pick up any hard cover book and you'll see that the first page is glued to the cover. Next is probably a blank page, then a title page, and maybe pages for a dedication and a table of contents. Chapter 1, page 1, in hardbound books is often page 13. What this means is that you'll need to put in a second set of numbers—the "real" numbers your readers will eventually see. To avoid confusion with the two numbering sequences, we use different colors for each.

ORIGINAL NUMBER CIRCLED

If you're thinking about obtaining a copyright when you plan your book, you can call the 24-hour Copyright Office hotline to request information and forms: (202) 707-9100.

Under current law, an originator of any work is automatically protected. What an

originator needs is a way of proving owner-
ship as of a certain date. All the Copyright
Office does is hold copies of your books and
a signed form you've filled out. To get a copyright, you'll need to:

1. request information and forms

2. put a copyright notice in your book (on the
   back of the title page in the exact form
   required)

3. send two copies of your finished book to
   the Copyright Office along with a fee (cur-
   rently $20)

Step 2:
Putting Copy on Long Strips

Unless you're using the kind of equipment that
composes pages for you, we suggest putting

your copy on long strips. When you've given your long strips the final proofreading, it's good to photocopy the original strips and save them in mint condition to use later.

door!
am I
trapped? Wh
to become of
me, a poor
orphan, all al
in the world?
Will I starv
before I can
bind my firs
novel... and
get the recogn
I so richly
deserve?

While doing your tentative layout with the photocopies, if you're including artwork or music, you'll want to estimate the size. (Or maybe you'll already have copies of the art/music in front of you, shrunk and stretched to several different sizes.)

To fasten your cutouts to each page of your dummy and still be able to keep shifting them around, you can use rubber cement or a small

waxer. (A waxer costs about $40 at an office supply store. It puts tiny wax dots on the back of your cutouts so they'll stay where you position them on your dummy.) Actually, we'll probably use transparent tape when making our first dummy.

If you want to be sure all your lines are straight, you can use folded graph paper to make the dummy. But for your first dummy, straight lines aren't important. (Be careful if you decide to use graph paper, because some kinds are made so the lines will show.)

When we're doing our final layout later, we'll not only use graph paper, but we'll also use a non-reproducing blue pencil for our original numbers.

To do our final layout, we'll use a home-made lightbox. It's nothing more than a piece of glass on a wooden frame with a light bulb underneath. This is like holding a piece of paper up to a window to see the marks on the other side. We'll put a plastic sheet on top of the glass to diffuse the light.

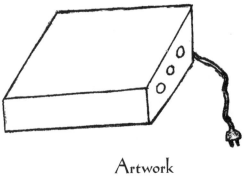

Artwork

Line drawings are easiest to handle. When we originally made the dummy for our book, after numerous sessions with the artist, we just glued her pictures where we wanted them.

Clip art is the term given to the simple drawings often found and reproduced in copy shops, and it includes borders and spacers (the kind often used in advertisements and flyers). Usually, you pay nothing to use them but the copying charges. Samples:

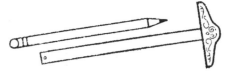

Rub-on and stick-on letters are handy for headings, and come in many different sizes and type styles. The letters on pages 18 and 19 are rub-on letters.

You've probably noticed that we keep mentioning using copiers for printing your book instead of getting the pages printed at a print shop. For black and white, we can tell no difference in the quality of printing, but the difference in cost is what makes us choose copiers for making just a few copies.

Colored pictures can either be printed at copy shops or print shops, but they're expensive, sorry to say.

Black-and-white photographs need to be screened at a print shop. For copy machine work, screening higher than 65 dots per inch isn't recommended.

Step 3: Preparing to Copy the Book's Tentative Pages

When our first dummy is complete (or mostly so) it's time to take it apart. We do this so we can get our tentative pages ready for the copy machine.

Before going to the copy shop, we use transparent tape to fasten the unfolded sheets together to prepare 8½" x 11" sheets to be copied.

Since our originals will have printing on both sides of each sheet, the finished sheets must be the same (with the right copy back to back). Here's what your first sheets will look like.

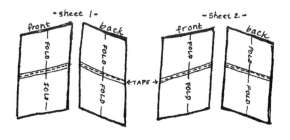

It doesn't matter that the transparent tape marks will show, as both original and "real" numbers will also show. (You don't need a non-reproducing blue pencil for the original numbers until the final photocopying.)

NOTE: Some copiers don't make copies exactly the same size as the original. All you need to do to check this is to hold your original to the light and compare it with that from the machine. Especially if you're working with small pages, you'll be awfully happy you checked on this before you did your final printing.

When you're through with your copying at the copy shop, if you need to use a paper cutter, you'll probably find one there.

At last, you're ready to fold your printed sheets and arrange the signatures.

Step 4: Final Copies

When you can stop admiring your tentative dummy (or dummies) and have made all the changes you're going to make, you're ready to take your original copy and lay out pages for final copying. (You won't be shifting copy around now, because by this time you've determined exactly where each piece is to go.)

Instead of taking the $8^1/_2$" x 11" sheets to the copier with the print on both sides of each sheet as before, we prefer to lay out each sheet so there's nothing on the back. It's just easier to see what we've got for final checking.

To avoid confusion when we're making the final copies (so we can get the right pages back to back), we'll check **our original page numbers** with this chart. If it seems confusing on your first reading, it will be clear when you look at your own dummy. You'll see that the pages are on front and back as we're showing here.

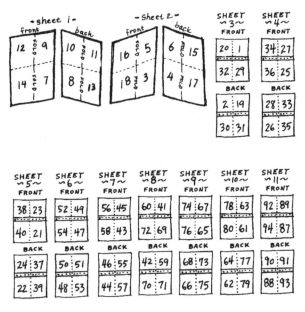

SHEET ~12~ FRONT	SHEET ~13~ FRONT	SHEET ~14~ FRONT	SHEET ~15~ FRONT	SHEET ~16~ FRONT	SHEET ~17~ FRONT	SHEET ~17½~ FRONT
96 : 85	100 : 81	118 : 103	114 : 107	132 : 129	136 : 125	140 : 121
98 : 83	120 : 101	116 : 105	112 : 109	134 : 127	138 : 123	

BACK	BACK	BACK	BACK	BACK	BACK	BACK
86 : 95	82 : 99	104 : 117	108 : 113	130 : 131	126 : 135	122 : 139
84 : 97	102 : 119	106 : 115	110 : 111	128 : 133	124 : 137	

We're still a long way from doing the final layout. We're working now with a three-ring binder, taping in finished pages of earlier chapters.

We're using the binder so we can see what the reader will see, two pages at a time. And proofreading is easy.

As long as we keep the original numbers on each page, we won't have any trouble laying out pages in the right places for final copying.

You may want to get paper for your final printing at a stationary store instead of a copy shop. Most paper today is made with chemicals that guarantee the paper's disintegration within a relatively short time (as compared with earlier papers, which sometimes lasted for hundreds of years). Thirty years is usually the estimated time for disintegration to occur, but there are many factors that cause differences in decomposition time. Everyone agrees that even protection from heat, light, or air won't stop the process. As you can guess, considerable research is being done at the Library of Congress to find a way of neutralizing the destructive chemicals, but without success so far. In the meantime, more and more paper mills are being converted so they can produce acid-free (alkaline) paper. And some publishers are now using the new paper exclusively. Unfortunately, the current retail price of acid-free paper is about double that of other paper.

When all your bookmaking decisions are behind you, your pages printed and bound, and your celebration is over, there's certainly one thing left: A deeper-than-ever appreciation for every human being throughout the ages who has ever had a part in producing books.

8

SUGGESTIONS FOR GROUP PROJECTS

No, we're not going to be giving you tips for assembly-line production, as we think you'll enjoy discovering them yourself. But we want to make just one point here.

Evidently, it's extremely difficult with most groups to allow time for the confusion and brainstorming inherent in group activities. To compensate, we suggest that you deliberately build into your plans a way to slow down the action. Sounds crazy? Maybe it is.

This suggestion comes from a favorite theory of ours about people who finish projects and those who only start them. At first glance it might seem that finishers are the ones who are most determined to reach a certain goal. Our experience is that the opposite is true: Finishers are those who most enjoy the process.

What is it that helps participants enjoy any group process? We think it's being truly involved, and that's especially important in the early information-gathering and discussion phase.

For a bookmaking project, for example, extensive practice time in handbinding blank books would guarantee a natural flow of brainstorming. (Corrugated cardboard covers? Tooled leather? Yard sale fabrics? Taking orders and making books for others? Compiling members' poems?...favorite recipes?...children stories?)

Let's pretend we're with a group of women planning to produce some books, and one of them has just presented the following book idea.

Two people meet another couple after work and decide to cook dinner together. No one has had time for advanced planning. And no one has spent hours in a kitchen. What if the four people had access to a truly wonderful book [produced by our group, of course] called *The Four Cooks Book*?

First the four cooks would choose a menu, preferably by numbers (or some method that would completely by-pass soul searching). Menus might be chosen for short preparation time, or they might be more appropriate for a rainy Sunday afternoon (maybe using masa harina to make tortillas, the kind that can sometimes be flattened between two bread boards laid out on a kitchen floor). Or menus might be grouped according to the kind of market the cooks might visit to do their shopping. Or an ideal book might call only for basic ingredients found in any supermarket.

With the book in hand, the cooks would read the preliminary instructions on the cover. (The book might be plastic wrapped so no one would know in advance what's inside.)

At the grocery store, cooks (assigned by number?) would each go to a different section of the market. By this time the book would have been opened (with proper ceremony, no doubt), and the shopping instructions read. Then after the cooks made their purchases, they would meet beyond the cash registers.

In this ideal book, the instructions would be so ideal that each person could spend approximately the same amount of money...and there'd be no leftovers.

Once inside the mutually agreed upon kitchen (or one chosen by lot?), no host or hostess would have any more responsibility than any other cook (except maybe to point out the location of utensils).

It's possible that each cook's instructions would be so wonderfully written that they'd automatically be read aloud.

Or things could go in the opposite direction, with maybe some cooks sworn to secrecy. For example, one cook might have the assignment of preparing fortune cookies for baking (the kind that are purchased flat). Maybe a helpful author has included a few suggested fortunes just in case the designated cook gets writer's block.

Hmmm...what about putting the suggested fortunes in a sealed envelope sewn in with the signatures? [Brainstorming again, we can already see mystery stories in handbound books, with the who-dun-it cleverly concealed until the last minute.]

How about the cooks enacting a mystery while they cook, with each one choosing one of four suggested roles? (Not really in costume, maybe, unless it's only a token costume accessory, like a sash. Or how about a cap concealing a knife? Or a bowtie with a crevice the exact size of a vial of poison?)

Let's listen in as the group brainstorms:

Why don't we skip the cookbook and just write a mystery about four people cooking together?

We could bind clues to go in sealed envelopes inside the mystery story…at just the right points. This would be like reading a book filled with puzzles, and readers wouldn't have to wait for the last page to find they'd been on the wrong track the whole time. With our book, readers wouldn't keep on reading unless they'd solved each puzzle...guaranteeing that they'd stay on track.

I've been thinking; It's families coming home together after work and school that need *The Four Cooks Book*. You know how it is. Usually there's one person giving the orders, and all the peasants are supposed to obey him or her (and instead the peasants are frantically trying to escape). With *The Four Cooks Book*, the roles would be chosen by number, so there'd be equal jobs for equal cooks—no bosses and no peasants—maybe even with penalties for those who interfere with another's territory.

Hey, this year why don't we just write a book about how we're going to write a book? We'll sell the books to our families and friends at the fall bazaar. And the following year we'll do another book...and each year there'll be great suspense about what book we're going to produce next, with maybe a prize for anyone who guesses it.

I've got it. Let's do something they'd never guess, do what I've always wanted to do. Let's write a book in secret code. I'd love it if someone would write such a book for me. Here, look at this: I've got something in code right here. Don't try to make sense of the pictures. Each one just represents a letter of the alphabet. In

about two seconds you'll probably figure out at least one of the letters.

Next week we can bring our most
unusual bookmaking ideas and mate-

rials. We could even make books with hollow covers for secret documents.

And I'm always wondering why there can't be blank books that would actually hold a pen or pencil.

Maybe we should think more about the kind of book each of us would like to see written...for ourselves. Wonder what our grandparents would have written if they'd been sitting around and decided to write a book about what each person had done during any one day?

Who knows where the discussion went from this point

We're just suggesting that groups are generally more likely to have fun and produce better books if they don't proceed in the traditional way: Setting hard deadlines too early, then relying on just a few people to carry the project over the finish line.

9

A WORD ABOUT PUBLISHING

*Y*ou may be wondering why authors would ever want to publish their own books. Or maybe you're thinking the opposite: Why would authors, especially the ones who believe they've created valuable works, ever hand their creations over to strangers?

We think it's been too long that authors thought the only route to getting published was by expecting strangers to take their work. And their expectations are sad to see. One large publisher, recently quoted in the press, said that his company had only published one unsolicited manuscript in 25 years.

If we don't like playing in a game with that kind of odds, what are the alternatives? We see two, and one of them is ugly.

When authors get too many rejection letters and become discouraged, they may answer an ad from a so-called vanity press publisher. And maybe they'll be persuaded to pay to have their books published. What's wrong with that? Actually, just about everything.

Vanity press and subsidy press (interchangeable terms) are companies that do what's called no-risk publishing. Because they collect authors' money in advance of printing, such publishers don't need to make their money producing saleable books.

If innocent authors don't know that publishing is mostly selling, they've walked into a trap: Knowledgeable book dealers instantly recognize vanity press books...and instantly shun them.

By far the best alternative to begging or paying strangers to take our works, from our point of view, is to do the publishing ourselves.

Did you know that all you have to do to get started in publishing is to declare yourself a publisher? You don't even need a book in hand. That's because publishing covers the entire process of taking a glimmer from someone's brain to converting it into a book that readers may enjoy discussing. It's possible that you're in an early phase of publishing right now and just don't recognize it.

We're serious. You can have some letterheads printed as soon as you've chosen a name for your company. (Think what those letterheads can do for your morale.)

You certainly don't have to worry about one publisher's complaint (reported in *Publishers Weekly*) that entry into publishing is at the curbstone level. Too bad! When big publishers can spend hundreds of thousands of dollars promoting just one title, they can't really be too worried about our entry into the competition, can they?

If our books sell well enough, larger publishers (with more cash for promotions) may decide to push our little jewels up the ladder. Richard Nelson Bolles self-published *What Color Is Your Parachute?* for two years before he passed it on to a larger publisher.

It's true that there's a big gap between giving away a few books and "going commercial." Publishing, and especially selling through bookstores, is gambling.

There's terrific competition for shelf space, and publishers are so desperate to get their books in stores that they usually agree to take back all unsold books for full credit.

According to a recent article on publishing, it's estimated that there are more books in transit between publishers and bookstores, at any one time, than there are on the shelves of all the bookstores put together. Sometimes books stay in bookstores just a few weeks before they're abandoned to make space for newer books (the ones always expected to sell better).

It's easy to see why bookstores don't want to carry books until buyers are asking for them. But it's also easy to see that buyers usually don't ask for books they haven't seen in bookstores.

One way it's possible to minimize the gamble of entering publishing is to start small. And it's best to identify in advance a well-defined market of eager book buyers.

Impossible? Not really. We hear of people who bind family histories and sell copies at family reunions. (Some of the books we've seen are double the size of this book and beautifully bound in doe suede cloth. The titles were put on in gold leaf.) From what we hear, bookbinders return to reunions each year with more books on more branches of the family...and place the books in buyers' outstretched hands.

As for our particular publishing company, it came to life when one of the authors of this book was burning with something to say. (This was while she was preparing to become a family counselor.)

At the time the small-press movement was expanding, she discovered, along with thousands of others, that writing is a lot more fun when combined with the power to get the words out.

Her motto at that time was an Ashleigh Brilliant quote: "I never thought so much would happen that I never thought would happen."*

When this book was first written, we at the Bookery Publishing Company were looking back over more than 250 talk shows and seminars, and this was our sixth book. We can't imagine any better route (available to us, anyway) for finding so much pleasure.

But publishing is always scary, as each decision carries a financial risk. When we published our first hardbound edition of this

---

* Pot-Shot No. 856 from *Pot-Shots and Brilliant Thoughts*, Ashleigh Brilliant Epigrams, used by permission of the author, Ashleigh Brilliant, 17 West Valerio St., Santa Barbara, CA 93101. Send $1 for catalog.

book, for example, we were extremely nervous about the dust jacket design. We thought it would be heaven to turn it over to an experienced art department. But would we have done so if we could have? Hard to say.

Some years ago, after we'd discovered handbinding, we recognized it as a means for fellow publishers to start small. Copy machines that would print on both sides of the paper had just come out about that time.

What this meant to us was that by doing handbinding and using a copy machine, we could produce 100 copies of our book to explain the process. Before we were through, even though we'd gone to offset printing instead of copy machine work, we'd produced 3,800 handbound books.

Today it's much easier to put print on a page, and we think that more people than ever will appreciate learning handbinding. But a publisher's main job is to let potential readers know of a book's existence.

It's probably no surprise to you to learn that small publishers may spend 70 to 80 percent of a book's selling price on marketing and distribution. (If you found the first edition of this book in a store, we may have paid 65 percent of the selling price to a distributer to get it there.)

When we initially finished writing this book, we were thinking about the hardest part of entering a publishing venture: Working through our self-doubts about the value of our work. That process goes on and on, but there's still another obstacle: Finding the courage to ask for others' evaluation of our work.

We're going to tell you how we've learned to minimize the pain of this process.

1. We first show our manuscript to a person who is both a friend and an author. We want someone who knows that an author's creative urge can disappear instantly with just one wrong word. (When the fun is gone, why write?)

2. We make sure we do enough thinking in advance to be able to tell the other person exactly the kind of feedback we want. It's the work's overall merit that we're nervous about. Shall we put it back in the drawer? Does it have any possibilities...at all?

3. We like it best if the other person will read the manuscript entirely without a pen or pencil in hand. We want to avoid getting little notes like, "I'd have said it this way" or "Why not use this example instead of that?" (Evidently it's awfully hard for some people to understand that even their

greatest ideas, offered at the wrong time, can be perceived as intolerable static.)

4. It takes another author to realize that the reason we write is that we have something that seems important for us to say.

5. We think getting feedback on our "baby's" overall worth is most tolerable if comes in sandwich form (a very thin filling between two strong, positive "overall" statements).

"Overall, I find it fascinating reading, and I especially like the way you handled...And that line about...

The only time I got a little confused was...

I think you're doing a great job. Just getting this kind of thing out for discussion is terrific. It's really going to be interesting to see where you go from here."

6. No matter how carefully the sandwich is prepared, or how much we truly want the feedback and believe we're prepared for it, we expect it to be hard to digest.

7. Because we know that editors sometimes have trouble saying things they perceive as negative, we think it's wise to take feedback silently and only later decide what to do with it.

8. We ask an editor to do no rewriting at all, as we just want direction where our rewriting is needed. Maybe we'll later initiate discussions only on the work's content or maybe only on the mechanics of the writing. But the time will be of our choosing, after we've worked through our doubts about the work's value...and after we're comfortable enough we can truly listen. (We weren't being obnoxious earlier, we just weren't able to listen yet.)

9. At some point we'll welcome another person's offer to double check our grammar, punctuation, and spelling. And it's certainly great when fresh eyes are available for proofreading.

10. Depending on the purpose of any particular work, we may decide to get more editing, whether professional or otherwise. But we also know that if we're willing to repeatedly let our manuscript cool off, and repeatedly return to it, eventually we'll have no urge to change it.

It feels good when we're no longer thinking of our work as a "baby" that needs protecting. Rather, we're seeing our work as something mature and exciting. It's almost become a living thing, completely prepared to interact with readers. And that's what it's doing right this minute.

Resources

As a reference book for publishing information, we suggest Dan Poynter's book ***The Self-Publishing Manual: How to Write, Print & Sell Your Own Book***. Where do you get the bar code for your book cover? How do you get on talk shows? Poynter tells it all! Contact Para Publishing, P.O. Box 4232-890, Santa Barbara, CA 93140-4232, (805) 968-7277. If you're not ready to start your own company, you can learn more about your publishing options from Judith Appelbaum's ***How to Get Happily Published***, HarperCollins Publishers, Inc., 10 East 53rd Street, New

York, NY, 10022, (800) 331-3761. In both Poynter's and Appelbaum's books you'll find excellent lists of resources for publishers.

At your library's reference desk, you can probably find ***Books in Print*** and the ***Subject Guide to Books in Print, Forthcoming Books*** and the ***Literary Marketplace***. For information on reference books and to order ***Publisher's Weekly*** and ***Library Journal***, contact: R.R. Bowker, 121 Chanlon Rd., New Providence, NJ 07974, (800) 521-8110. We use ***Small-Time Operator: How to Start Your Own Small Business, Keep Your Books, Pay Your Taxes, and Stay Out of Trouble!*** Author Bernard Kamoroff has 435,000 copies in print and still runs his own publishing company. Obtain a copy of this book by contacting: Bell Springs Publishing, Box 640, Bell Springs Rd., Laytonville, CA 95454, (707) 984-6746. We suggest ***Book Publicity for***

Authors, by Larry J. Rochester (media pro-
ducer, talk show host, and publicist): Sunset
Hill Publishing Co., Box 444, Fall River
Mills, CA 96028, (916) 335-2441. You may
also want to check out two organizations:
Publishers Marketing Association, 2401
Pacific Coast Hwy., #102, Hermosa Beach,
CA 90254, (310) 372-2732, and the **Pacific
Center for the Book Arts**, P.O. Box 8701,
Oakland, CA 94662-8701.

Index

artwork, 76
  binding children's,
    11, 21
  black and white
    photos, 80
  clip art, 79
  color pictures, 79
  line drawings, 78
  rub-on letters, 79

binding
  different sizes, 36
  multiple copies, 69

cardboard (chipboard),
  28-29, 31, 37, 39, 42

cloth, cover, 25, 30, 31,
  40, 42, 66-67

copyright, 72-73

cover guide, 27, 29, 31, 37

dedication page, 71

distributing books, 109

dummy, 70, 76, 77, 78,
  80, 83

end papers, 27-28, 31, 66

evaluating manuscripts,
  109-113

glue, white, 25, 31, 32, 33

gluing, 39, 41, 44
  end papers, 67
  pages to cover, 61-65
  spine, the, 58-60

graph paper, 77

ideas, 5-12, 20, 89-100

laying out, 76, 77, 78, 85

layout chart, 84-85

Library of Congress, 87

marketing books, 109

materials, 24-33

nonreproducing blue
  pencil, 77

pages
  folding, 34-36
  numbering, 71-83, 86

paper, 26, 27, 31, 87

photocopying
  final pages, 83
  preparing book pages
  for, 80-82

publishing resources,
  114-116

rubber cement, 76

self-publishing, 101, 103

sewing chart, 57

sewing pages, 41-49,
  50-57

signature(s), 35, 70

table of contents, 71

thread, 25, 31

title page, 71

transparent tape, 77

wax paper, 25, 31

vanity press, 102

Order Form

	QTY	AMOUNT

Starter Packet—$4.75   ____ $ _____

Complete material for binding a 140-page book
(5³/₄"x4¹/₄"). Includes: Cardboard for cover/spine,
paper (for pages, cover guide and end papers),
glue, wax paper, needle, thread, and cloth.
(shipping weight 9 oz.)

Cardboard Only   ____ $ _____

For 5 books—$2.50 (shipping weight 12 oz.)
For 10 books—$4.50 (shipping weight 23 oz.)

Gift Packet—$15   ____ $ _____

Gift-wrapped box containing one copy of
Hey Look, I Made a Book!, plus one Starter Packet.
Please indicate theme for gift wrap, name and
address of recipient, and the message you'd
like us to enclose.(Shipping weight 21 oz.)

Hey Look...I Made a Book!—$7.95   ____ $ _____

New paperback edition. (Shipping weight 12 oz.)

Subtotal $ _____

Sales Tax (CA only) add 7.25% $ _____

Shipping (See next page for shipping charges.) $ _____

Total $ _____

Shipping charges

up to 1 lb.—$2.50
each additional lb.—add $1.00

Send check or money order payable to:

Handbinders' Supplies
3939 Heron Lane
Cottonwood, CA 96022

For more information on additional supplies available or quantity discounts, ask for our free brochure.